YOU'RE IN LOVE WHEN...
300HE91-0
REVERSE FRONT ENDSHEET

You're In Love When...

You're In Love When...

By
Dean Walley

Hallmark Editions

Set in Baker Signet, a modified old style typeface
designed by Arthur Baker.
Typography by Hallmark Photo Composition.
Printed on Hallmark Eggshell Book paper.
Designed by Jay D. Johnson.

Copyright © 1971 by Hallmark Cards, Inc.,
Kansas City, Missouri. All Rights Reserved.
Printed in the United States of America.
Library of Congress Catalog Card Number: 71-164663.
Standard Book Number: 87529-231-3.

You're In Love When...

You're in love...
when love is in you.

You're in love...

when morning shines in
and starts a
"something's coming" feeling
racing back and forth
within you...

...and you can't wait to get out of bed,
 through the shower,
  around the breakfast,
   close to the one you love.

You're in love...

when you stop thinking
      about that face in the mirror
  and concentrate upon an image
      traced across your heart.

You're in love...

when you feel like writing a poem...

...when you feel,

    all of a sudden,

    that the two of you ARE a poem.

You're in love...

when you finally get the letter
 you've been waiting for...

...and you read it over and over
               and over again
         and check the back of each page
           to make sure
              you haven't missed anything...

...and then carry it
 around with you for months,
reading it again at odd moments
 just for reassurance
 even though
 you know every line by heart.

You're in love...

when you find
 that a park
 or a city street
 or a library
  can be a perfect place
   for lovers...

...when even a little room
>   over a shop
>   on a shabby street
>   seems just a door away
>> from heaven...
>   because the two of you are there.

You're in love...

when the hands on the clock
			seem to move too fast,
	and there is never
			enough time
				for togethering.

You're in love...

when
without even being asked the question
you find yourself saying
yes, yes, yes,
YES!

You're in love...

when you stop telling everyone
how much in love you are...

...and everyone begins to smile at you
with a look that says,
"How much in love you are!"

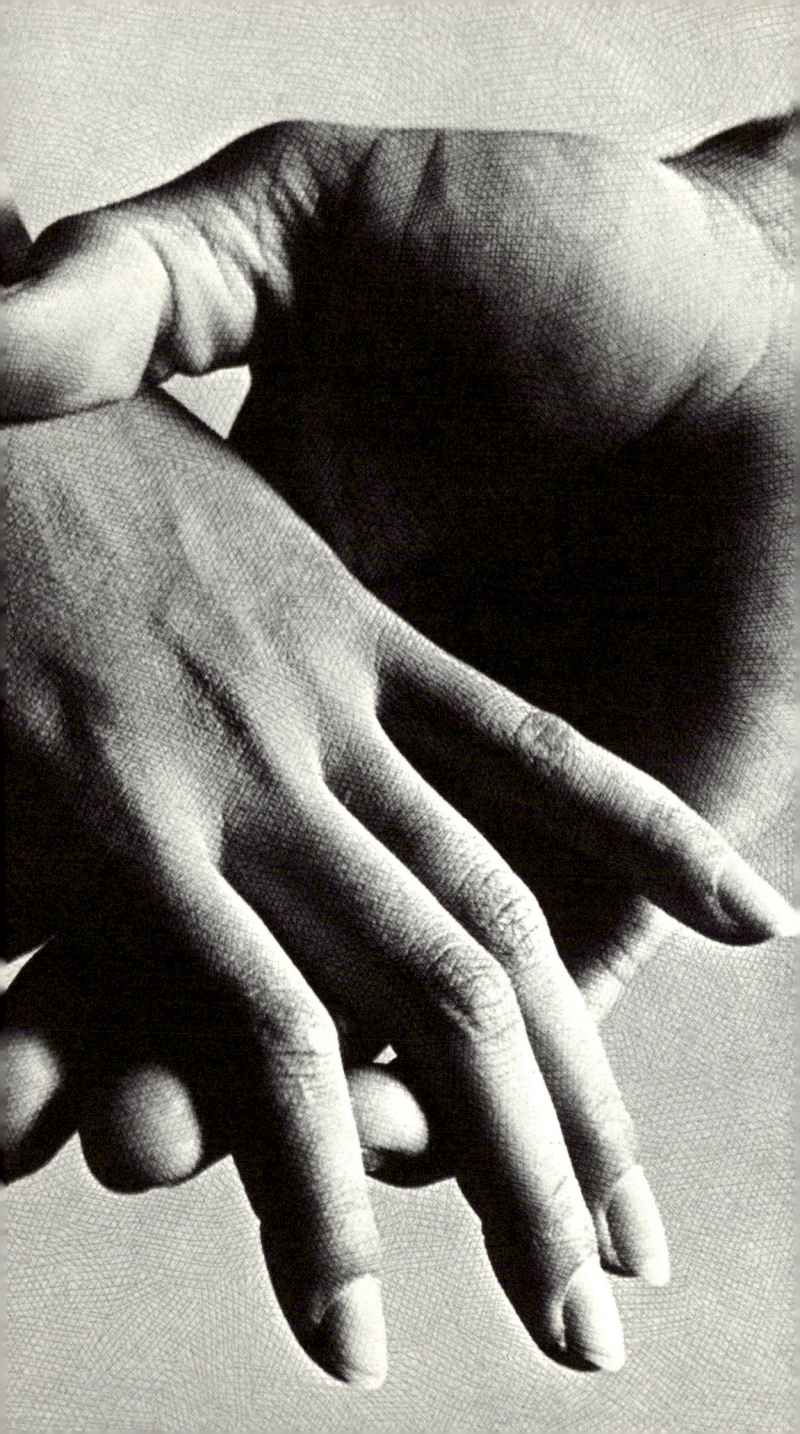

You're in love...

when staying home together
    REALLY IS
            better than going out...

...and your every meeting
            becomes
                a celebration...

...and all the things you do

are love.

You're in love…

when there is nothing more to prove…

...when
instead of trying to change each other...

...you think of ways to change yourself.

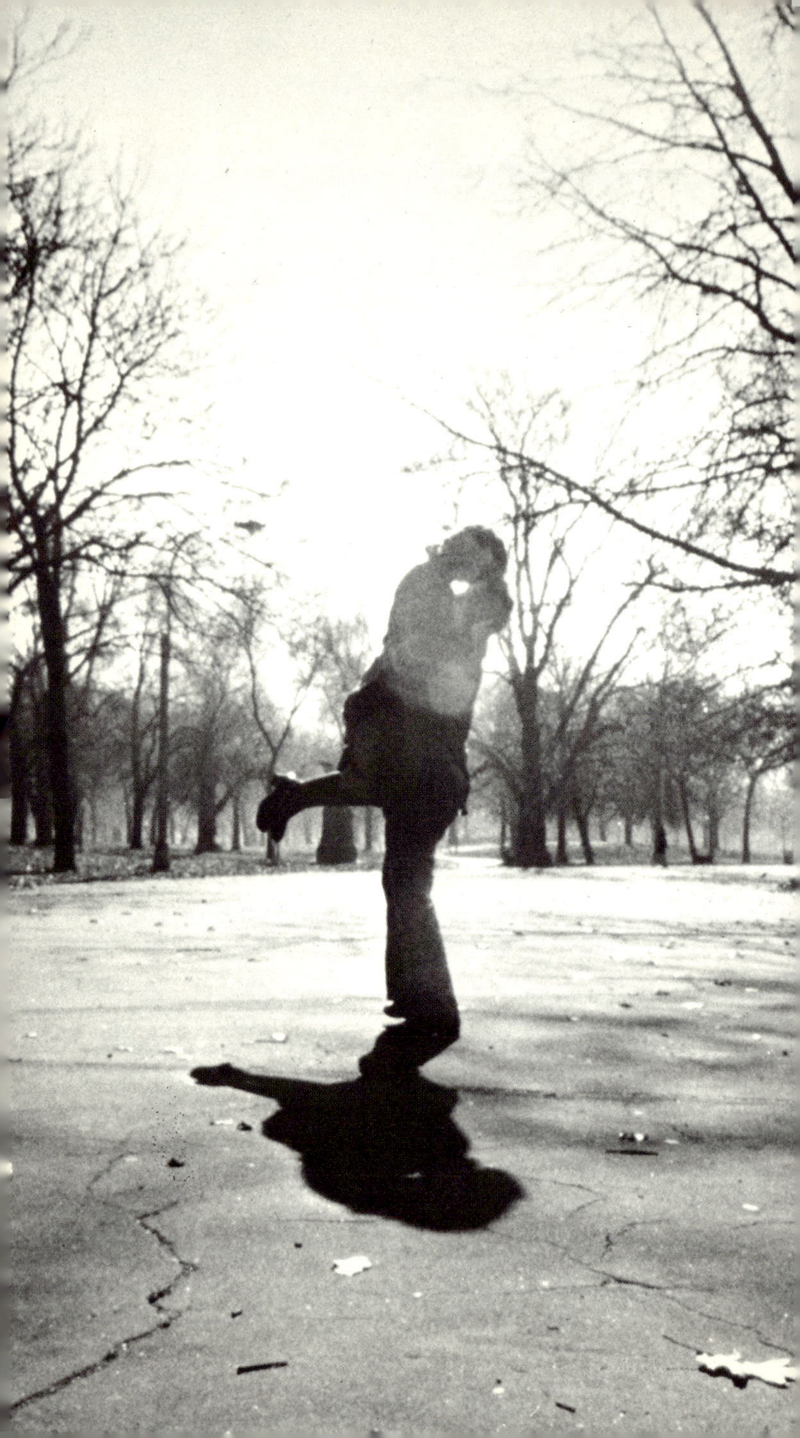

You're in love…

when you get that springtime feeling
    of expectancy
    and joy
on one of those ordinary days
    in February.

You're in love...

when you spend sunny nights
and starry days
together...

...and when desire has flamed
and gone,
leaving a quiet ember,
and you dream together
drifting on the surface
of sleep.

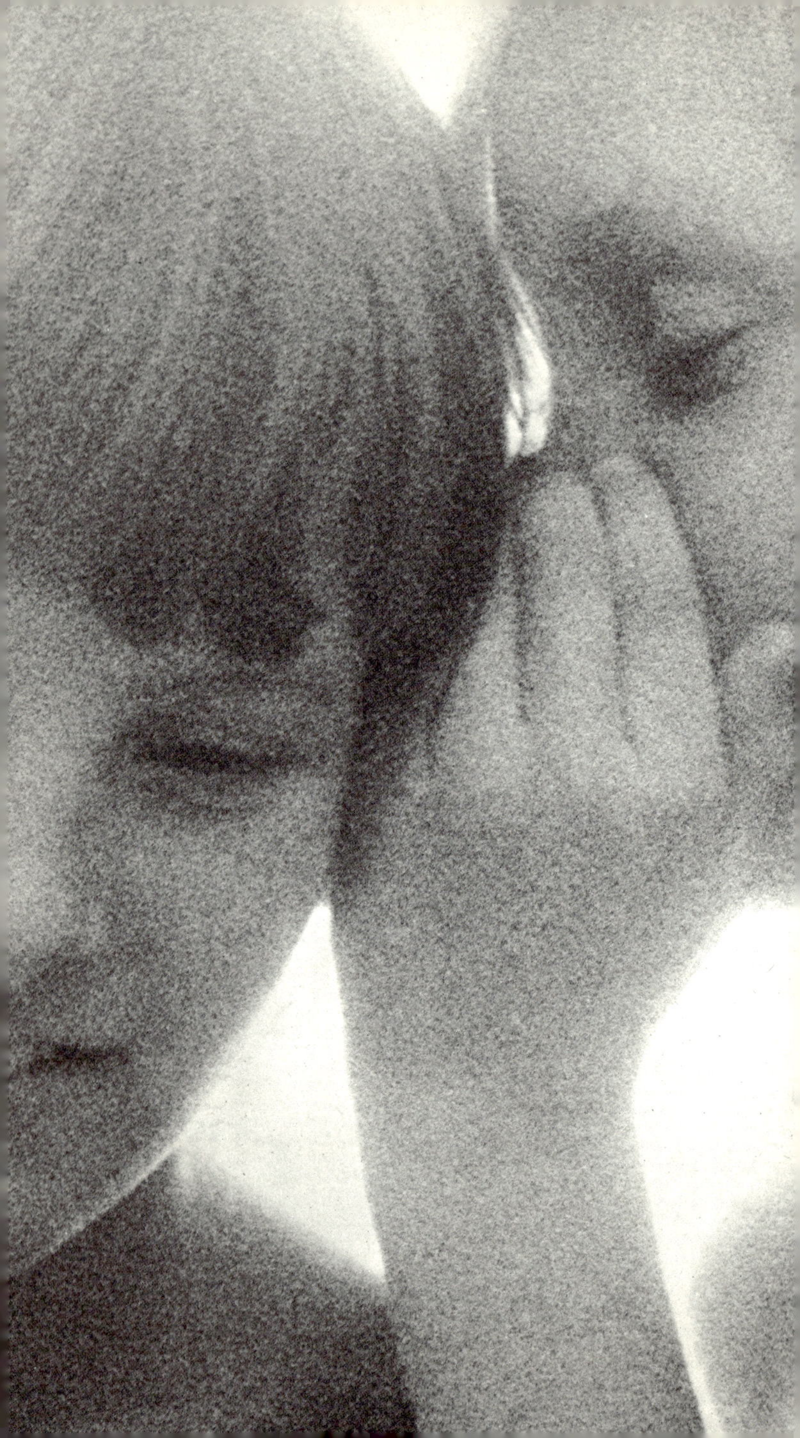

You're in love...

      when
by looking in the hiding places
    of another heart
    you manage to retrieve
          your innocence....

And when you're wise enough
   and strong enough
to admit
that you're never really sure of love...

...then

chances are

    love is sure of you.

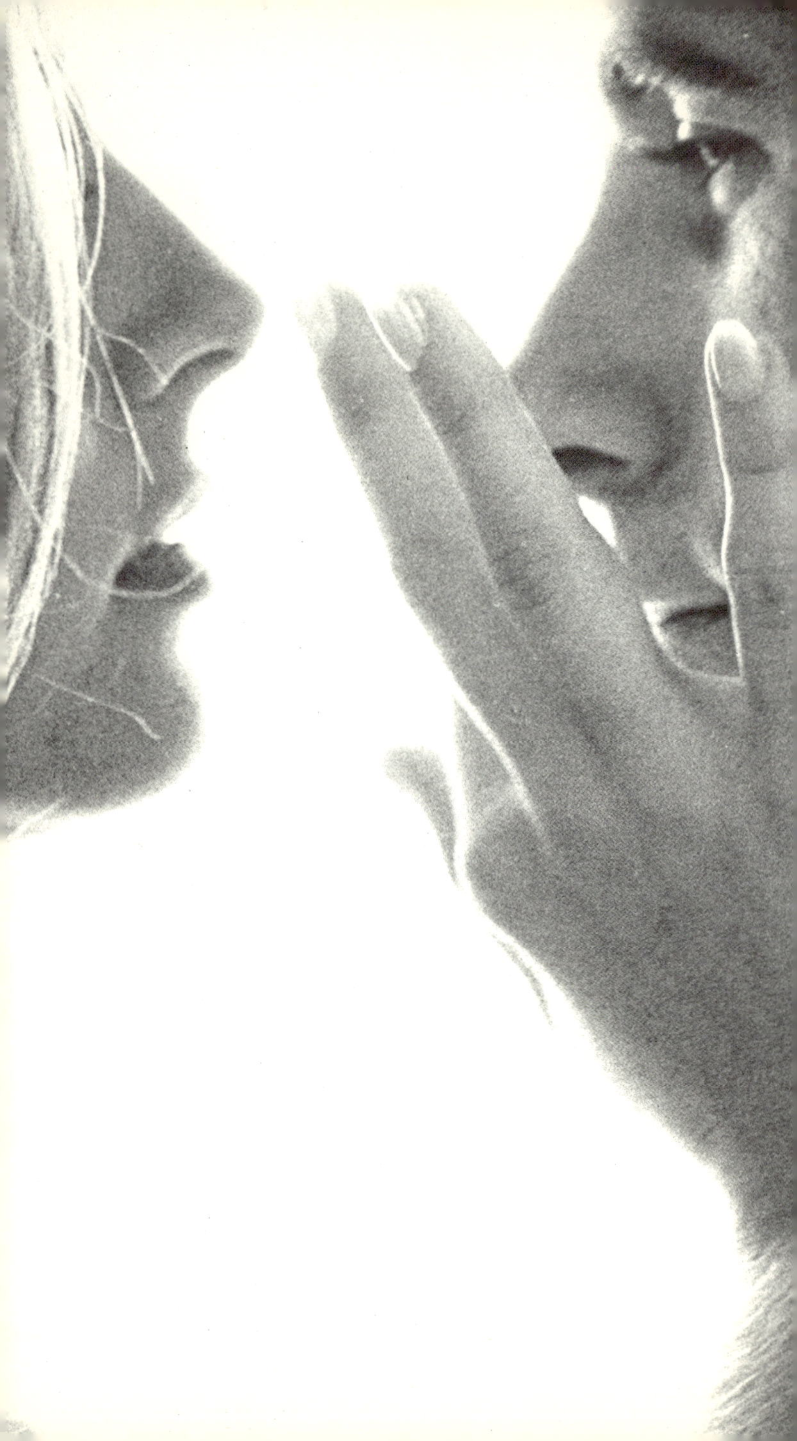

You're in love...

    when you see the sun,
        as if for the first time,
            perfected in another's eyes.

...when a glance holds more tenderness
than a thousand kisses...

...and two voices mingling in joy
    hold more passion
        than two bodies intertwined.

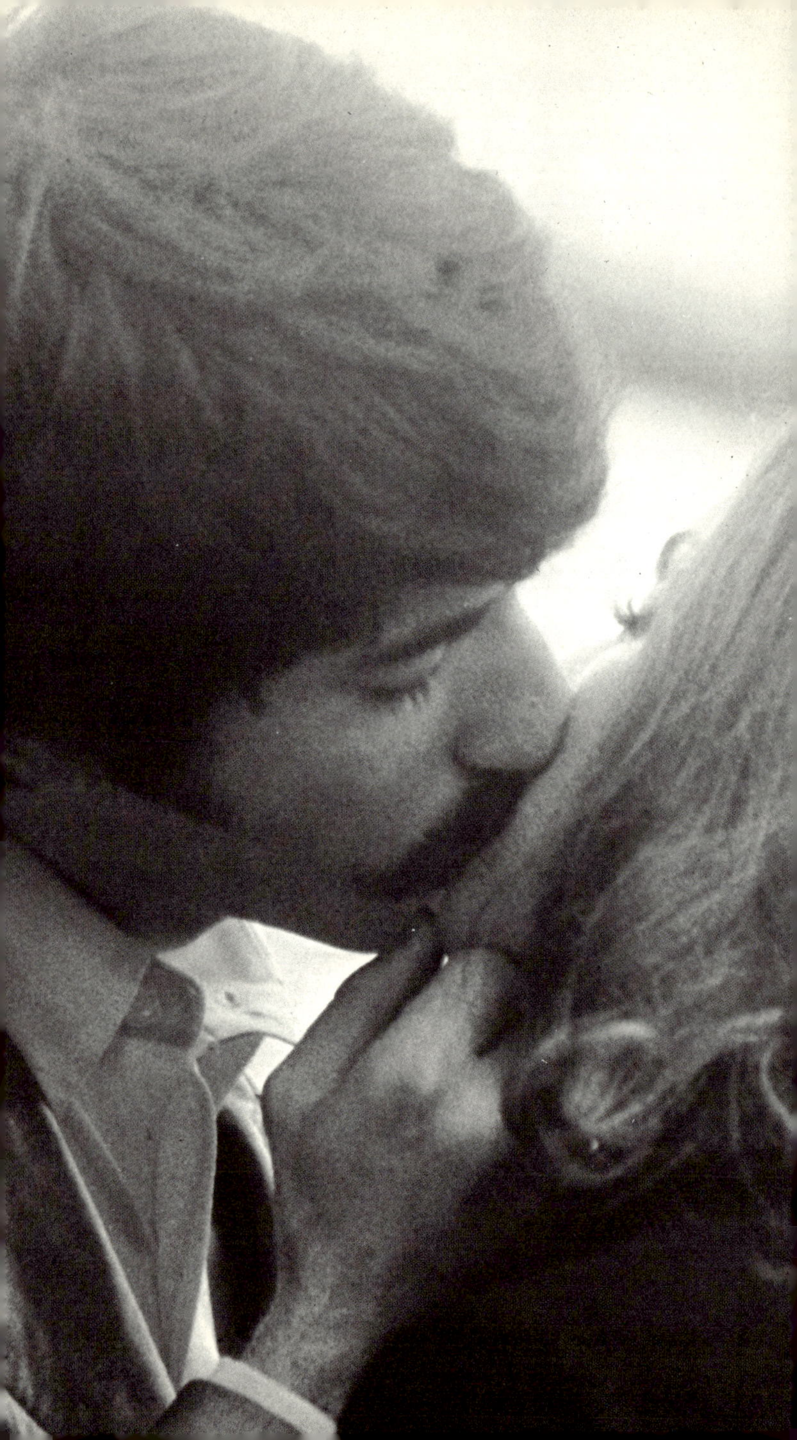

And when you somehow
feel all the sweetness and strength
of the love that is in you...

...then

it must be true...

        you are in love.